Rodrigo Rex

Analysing Wireless Networks with different IEEE 802.11 protocols

Rodrigo Rex

Analysing Wireless Networks with different IEEE 802.11 protocols

Performance analysis of point-to-point wireless networks with different IEEE 802.11 protocols

ScienciaScripts

Cover image: www.ingimage.com

This book is a translation from the original published under ISBN 978-613-9-64902-0.

Publisher:
Sciencia Scripts
is a trademark of
Dodo Books Indian Ocean Ltd. and OmniScriptum S.R.L publishing group

120 High Road, East Finchley, London, N2 9ED, United Kingdom
Str. Armeneasca 28/1, office 1, Chisinau MD-2012, Republic of Moldova, Europe
Printed at: see last page
ISBN: 978-620-7-79806-3

ACKNOWLEDGEMENTS

Firstly, I thank God, who is responsible for illuminating my personal, professional and academic life, giving me the strength and courage to move forward.

To my family, who are the basis of everything, especially my parents and my sister for always supporting and encouraging me.

I would also like to thank my girlfriend Beatriz Specht for all her patience, words of encouragement and trust in my life projects and the happy moments she gives me every day.

I would also like to thank the teachers at Univates who helped me during my degree, but especially my supervisor Edson Funke, who accompanied me and helped me to prepare this study in the best possible way.

And finally, thank you to my friends, simply for being great friends.

SUMMARY

Wireless computer networks are changing the way people work or relate to each other, in other words, they are present in our lives and, it seems, increasingly so. This paper analyses wireless computer networks by comparing the performance of the IEEE 802.11 protocols currently on the market. To this end, a theoretical foundation was created, covering concepts from authors in the areas of computer networks and wireless networks. The method used for this study will be exploratory, where the information needed to analyse the data was collected through a bibliographical survey and a case study. It was concluded that protocols have evolved over the years, providing more capacity for wireless networks. It is believed that the results of this study can serve as a basis for domestic or organisational users when choosing to use a particular piece of wireless network equipment.

Keywords: Wireless networks, IEEE 802.11, Capacity.

SUMMARY

CHAPTER 1

INTRODUCTION

Computing is increasingly present in organisations and homes and is fundamental to speeding up processes, many of which are only possible through it, since computer processing capacity is constantly evolving and surprising us every day.

Uniting the capacity of computers through a network is the ideal scenario for a world that demands information and action in real time. Computer networks are changing the way people work, study or relate to each other, they are already present in our lives and it seems that they will become increasingly so (TANENBAUM; WETHERALL, 2011).

Basically, computer networks are associated with two types of physical media: wired networks and wireless networks. Each has its own characteristics, but they generally coexist and complement each other in organisational or residential environments.

Wired networks have been used for years and for a long time they were the only way to connect computers to the internet, but they are not very practical when it comes to mobility, since devices that use this type of connection need cables connected to them all the time.

Wireless networks have come to simplify and promote access to computer networks and the internet. As well as adding a series of new devices to the global network such as mobile phones, tablets and notebooks, more and more new equipment is compatible with the standard, giving rise to the concept of the internet of things. Soon we will have countless devices in our homes and organisations directly connected to the internet, automating and simplifying our lives (TANENBAUM; WETHERALL, 2011).

In order to guarantee the functionality of wireless networks, the IEEE (Institute of Electrical and Electronics Engineers) 802.11 protocol, generically known as Wi-Fi, was created in 1997 to govern standards and provide interoperability between different manufacturers of equipment designed for this technology. Since then, the protocol has evolved in line with technological needs. The first versions had very limited traffic capacities. Today, wireless networks can provide transfer rates of over 1 GB per second. The increasing use of Wi-Fi networks is fuelling the advancement of this technology, which is used all over the world (TANENBAUM; WETHERALL, 2011).

In mid-2013, the IEEE 802.11ac wireless network protocol was launched. Since then, manufacturers have been launching equipment that operates with this technology, which brings a series of benefits over the old protocols, providing more information traffic capacity and greater network coverage, as well as correcting and eliminating errors from previous technologies (TANENBAUM; WETHERALL, 2011).

1.1 Delimitation of the study

A bibliographical study will be carried out, as well as an in-depth analysis of the relevant technical aspects of a wireless network connection, in addition to analysing the data collected using network auditing tools. The aim is to verify the main differences in performance between current wireless network protocols.

1.2 Research problem

Organisational and personal needs drive the evolution of technologies. With this in mind, wireless networks need to provide more and more capacity for the flow of data and information in real time. Knowing this, researchers are constantly evolving the standards and protocols that govern this technology, providing new quality and speed parameters.

This research therefore asks: What is the difference in performance between the IEEE 802.11a/b/g/n/ac wireless network protocols?

1.3 Objectives

Through the questions of this study, the objectives described below were defined.

1.3.1 General objective

The general objective of this study is to determine the difference in performance between the wireless network protocols of the IEEE 802.11 family and its sub-standards, whose equipment is currently being marketed.

1.3.2 Specific objectives

In order to achieve the main objective of this study, it is also necessary to look for:

a) Technically evaluate the performance of IEEE 802.11 a/b/g/n/ac wireless network protocols;

b) Compare the performance of IEEE 802.11 a/b/g/n/ac wireless network protocols;

c) Check under what circumstances the use of one protocol or another is justified;

1.4 Justification

This study is justified by the belief that it will contribute to the academic, personal and organisational spheres. From an academic point of view, through searches carried out between July and September 2015, no similar works were found in the databases, thus guaranteeing a relevant contribution to the area.

In the organisational and personal spheres, the growth in the use of wireless network technology is evident in our homes, organisations and public places. This great expansion in the use of technology is due to its practicality in terms of mobility and connectivity. However, there are parameters and limitations that must be addressed, as well as knowing the right time to migrate a wireless network from one protocol to another.

In order to justify investment in new equipment, it is necessary to analyse all the factors that influence decision-making, and in the case of technology, one of the main factors is the performance that the equipment provides. With the information resulting from this research, organisations, home users or academics will be able to analyse the benefits and limitations of the technology of each IEEE 802.11 protocol in their wireless networks.

1.5 Work structure

In order to achieve the proposed objectives, the work is structured in four chapters, as can be seen in Figure 1.

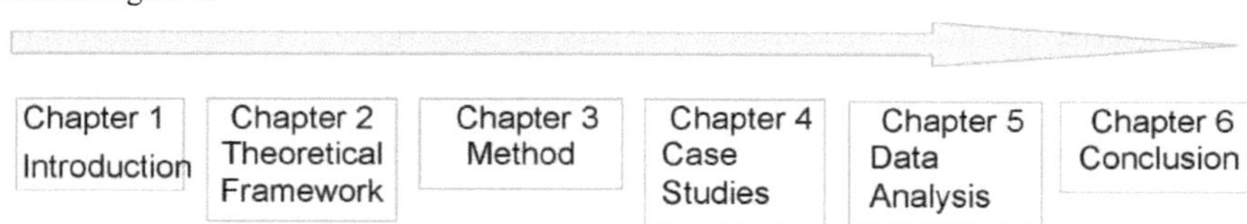

Figure 1 - Structure of the work

Source: prepared by the author.

Chapter 1 contextualises the topic and its relevance, as well as presenting the objectives, justifications and structure of the work. Chapter 2 examines the bibliography relating to the research topic. Chapter 3 presents the methodological procedures used to carry out the work. Chapter 4 presents the case study. Chapter 5 analyses the results of the scenarios studied. Chapter 6 contains the conclusions of the work.

At the end are the references of the works cited throughout the chapters, as well as the appendices that substantiated the research.

CHAPTER 2

THEORETICAL FRAMEWORK

This chapter covers the concepts and works that have already been published and that are necessary for grounding and contextualising the themes related to the research. Bearing in mind the main objective of this work, it is necessary to address the concepts of computer networks and wireless networks.

2.1 Computer networks

Computer networks are directly or indirectly linked to people's professional or social lives. Even without realising it, a large part of the population uses them in some way, whether for work or to communicate with friends and family, bringing countless benefits to people's lives and great evolution to organisations (FOROUZAN, 2008).

According to Tanenbaun and Watherall (2011), the old idea of a single computer meeting the needs of organisations has been replaced by another, where tasks are carried out by a set of autonomous computers, but interconnected through computer networks. Communication doesn't necessarily have to be done by wires; optical cables, microwaves, infrared waves or data communication satellites can also be used.

Two reference models were defined to meet the need to interconnect computers via networks, according to Forouzan (2008): the *OSI (Open Systems Interconnection) model and the TCP/IP (Transmission Control and Interconnection)* model.

Protocol/Internet Protocol) and are discussed below.

2.1.1 OSI model

With the emergence of the concept of interconnected computer networks, it became necessary to address the parameters required for them to function properly.

The OSI Reference Model (Open System Interconnection), which deals with the interconnection of systems open to communication with other systems, was developed by the ISO (International Standards Organisation) as a first step towards the standardisation of network protocols (TANENBAUM; WETHERALL, 2011).

The OSI Model is divided into 7 layers, each of which is explained below, according to Tanenbaum and Wetherall (2011).

2.1.1. 1Physical layer

The physical layer deals with the transmission of bits from one side to the other via a communication channel. It must ensure that if one side transmits a bit 0, the other must receive a bit 0 and not a bit 1. To do this, the electrical signals used to represent the bits must be aligned, how many nanoseconds they must last, questions about the start and end of the transmission and whether it can be simultaneous in both directions.

2.1.1.2 Data Link Layer

The task of the data link layer is to transform a physical communication channel into a line that appears to be free of transmission errors. To do this, it masks the real errors so that the network layer does not notice them, so the sending of data packets from a transmitter to a receiver must be confirmed

to maintain the reliability of communication, this is its fundamental role (TANENBAUM; WETHERALL, 2011).

2.1.1. 3Network layer

The network layer basically determines how data packets are routed from source to destination, the routes can be static or dynamic depending on the network design. If there are too many network packets at the same time sharing the same route, there can be congestion, which is also the responsibility of the network layer to deal with, helping with the quality of the data transmission service (TANENBAUM; WETHERALL, 2011).

2.1.1.4 Transport layer

The transport layer's job is to accept data, split it into smaller units if necessary and ensure that all the fragments reach the other end correctly. It is considered the true end-to-end layer, connecting the source to the destination.

2.1.1. 5Session Layer

It allows users on different machines to establish communication sessions, keeping track of who should be transmitting at any given time, preventing two parties from trying to perform the same critical operation at the same time and carrying out periodic checks on long transmissions to allow them to continue from where they were when a failure occurs.

2.1.1. 6Presentation Layer

Unlike the other layers below, which are concerned with the transmission of bits, the presentation layer is concerned with the syntax and semantics of

to make it possible for computers to communicate with different data representations (TANENBAUM; WETHERALL, 2011).

2.1.1.1 Application Layer

The application layer comprises a series of protocols needed by users, for example, protocols used for transferring e-mails, transmitting data or web pages.

2.1.2 TCP/IP model

According to Forouzan (2008), the TCP/IP model was developed before the OSI model, so its layers do not correspond exactly to the OSI model. Below is a brief explanation of the layers of the TCP/IP model, according to Forouzan (2008) and Tanenbaum and Wetherall (2011).

2.1.2.1 Physical and Link Layer

The documentation does not specify any exact actions for the Physical and Link layers, only that a host must connect to a network using a protocol that allows the transmission of IP packets. No specific protocol is mentioned for communication, supporting all standard and proprietary protocols for communication between hosts and networks.

2.1.2.2 Network Layer

The purpose of the Network layer or network link layer is to allow hosts to send packets on any network, guaranteeing that they will travel independently to their destination. Packets may even arrive in a different order to the one they were sent in, the role of reorganising them (if necessary) lies with the upper layers (FOROUZAN, 2008; TANENBAUM; WETHERALL, 2011).

2.1.2. 3Transport Layer

Very similar to the transport layer of the OSI model, in the TCP/IP model, two protocols control transmission; one of them, TCP (Transmission Control Protocol), prioritises the delivery of packets reliably and without errors, while the UDP (User Datagram Protocol) protocol prioritises transmission speed, but does not guarantee the receipt of the packet.

2.1.2.4 Application Layer

The application layer in the TCP/IP model incorporates the section, presentation and application layers of the OSI model. It is the highest level of the TCP/IP model and represents file transfer protocols (FTP), electronic mail (SMTP), host name mapping (DNS), web page search (HTTP), among many others.

2.2 Wireless computer networks

According to Tanenbaum and Wetherall (2011), wireless networks are constantly expanding, present in homes, organisations, universities and public places, providing practicality, agility and cost savings when installing and using computer networks to access internal networks or the Internet. Many users don't even realise the importance of wireless networks in their lives, due to the practicality with which they provide fast and secure connections.

The need to connect devices to the Internet without the use of cables led researchers in the mid-1990s to develop ways of achieving this goal. The most practical way would be to equip environments and access devices with shortwave radio transmitters and receivers (TANENBAUM; WETHERALL, 2011).

The choice of short-wave radio receivers quickly led to the

commercialisation of wireless networks by various companies. The problem was compatibility between devices, since a brand X transmitter wouldn't work with a brand Y receiver. To solve the interoperability problem, a wireless network standard was developed by the IEEE (Institute of Electrical and Electronics Engineers) committee, called IEEE 802.11, better known by the slang term Wi-Fi.

2.2. 1 IEEE802.11 family

The IEEE 802.11 standard is a set of norms and standards for transmission in wireless networks, guaranteeing interoperability between different equipment standards. The current standards governing wireless networks are described below.

2.2.1.1IEEE802 .11b

Approved in 1999, it uses the 2.4 GHz spectrum as its frequency band, working at rates of up to 11 Mbps, but in practice the protocol reaches a maximum speed of 5.9 Mbps using TCP and 7.1 Mbps using UDP (MORAES, 2010).

This standard is based on multipoint communication, where an Access Point communicates with one or more wireless network clients, establishing an average range of 30 to 90 metres, a factor that directly affects performance and the total number of users using a given channel (MORAES, 2010).

In outdoor environments and point-to-point configurations, using high-gain antennas, distances of up to eight kilometres can be reached (MORAES, 2010).

2.2.1.2IEEE802 .11a

Moraes (2010) states that approved in conjunction with 802.11b, the protocol

802.11a allows operation in bands of up to 54 Mbps, uses the 5 GHz spectrum and in practice delivers around 20 Mbps of transmission. There is no interoperability between the 802.11a and 802.11b protocols, as they work in two different frequency bands, unless the equipment is capable of working in two frequency bands.

The 5 GHz frequency band offers significant advantages, the main one being that the 2.4 GHz band is very overloaded, microwave ovens, cordless phones and countless other devices use the same band, plus the number of channels in the 5 GHz band is four to eight times greater (MORAES, 2010).

However, the 5 GHz band also has some disadvantages, since the frequency is higher, the range decreases, since the signal is more absorbed by walls and other solid objects, and the range ends up being 50 per cent less than in the 802.11b standard (MORAES, 2010).

2.2.1.3 IEEE802.11g

According to Moraes (2010), the 802.11g standard is an extension of the 802.11b standard, in fact there is compatibility between them, since the two work in the same frequency range, basically what differentiates one from the other is the fact that 802.11g works in a more efficient modulation, which allows a nominal transmission rate equal to the 802.11a standard, of 54 Mbps and effective of 19 Mbps but with the same signal range as the 802.11b standard, because they work in the same frequency range.

The compatibility of the 802.11b and 802.11g standards leads to some problems: the existence of stations working on 802.11b considerably reduces the performance of an 802.11g network. Although acceptance of the 802.11g standard has been high, this technology is subject to the same interference as 802.11b due to its extensive use of the 2.4 GHz spectrum. Devices working in this frequency range are susceptible to interference from other devices (MORAES, 2010).

2.2.1.4 IEEE802.11n

Moraes (2010) states that published in 2009, IEEE 802.11n aims to increase the speed obtained in previous standards from 54Mbps to up to 600Mbps, using up to 4 data channels, with 40MHz spacing between them.

The idea is to use the concept of MIMO (Multiple Imput Multiple Output), multiplexing and adding more antennas to data transmission, which considerably increases transmission capacity. Another factor that allows for greater bandwidth capacity is the fact that it can use a channel width of 40MHz, doubling the capacity of the old standards that used 20MHz (MORAES, 2010).

Advanced modulation techniques have allowed transfer rates to increase considerably compared to the old standards. Another feature is the backwards compatibility of the 802.11n protocol with its predecessors, but a mixed protocol network does not deliver the same capacity as a pure 802.11n network (MORAES, 2010).

2.2.1.5 IEEE802.11ac

Published in mid-2012, the 802.11ac protocol explores three fundamental and interrelated items in order to increase the transmission rate above 3Gb/s (PLAZA, 2014). These are:

- Increased bandwidth;
- Increased spectral efficiency;
- Improved signal-to-noise ratio.

The new protocol now uses bandwidths of up to 160 MHz, 4 times greater than the previous protocol, and new modulation techniques have been implemented to accommodate the increased transmission rate and allow for greater signal efficiency.

Another measure taken was the extinction of the 2.4 GHz spectrum in the 802.11ac protocol, which now exclusively uses 5 GHz channels, allowing for a greater number of channels, as well as being less polluted than 2.4 GHz.

2.2.2 Wave theory

When it comes to wireless networks, we have to address issues such as waves, frequencies, channels, signal, bandwidth, capacity, among others that are relevant and fundamental to the propagation of the transmission. The propagation process can be understood below (FLICKENGER et al., 2007).

2.2.2.1 Electromagnetic waves

Electromagnetic waves can be compared to a stone thrown into a pond. As soon as the stone hits the water, it generates a wave that propagates and attenuates as it travels through the pond. Wireless networks use electromagnetic waves to propagate data, they have a certain speed, frequency and wavelength, these properties are arranged as follows:

Speed = Frequency * Wavelength

The length of an electromagnetic wave is the distance measured from one point of the wave to the equivalent part of the next wave, and the frequency is the number of complete waves that propagate in a given period of time (FLICKENGER et al., 2007).

2.2.2.2 Electromagnetic spectrum

Electromagnetic waves exist in a wide range of frequencies and lengths, this range is called the electromagnetic spectrum. Wireless computer networks use frequencies between 2.400 and 2.495 GHz (with a wavelength of 12.5 cm) for the 802.11b, 802.11g and 802.11n protocols, while the spectrum in the 5.150 to 5.850 GHz range (with a wavelength of 5 and 6 cm) is used for the 802.11a, 802.11g, 802.11n and the new 802.11ac protocols.

2.2.2.3 Polarisation

Another property of electromagnetic waves is polarisation, which is defined by the antenna used in the wireless network. Basically, if the antenna is placed vertically, the waves move up and down, i.e. vertically, and the opposite occurs if the antenna is placed horizontally. Figure 2 illustrates the propagation of vertical and horizontal waves.

Figure 2 - Propagation of vertical and horizontal waves

Source: FLICKENGER et al. (2007, p. 13).

2.2.2.4 Bandwidth

Bandwidth is the measure of frequency variation and is closely related to the amount of data we can transmit within it - the higher the bandwidth, the more data we can transmit on the wireless connection (FLICKENGER et al., 2007).

2.2.2.5 Frequencies and channels

A 2.4 GHz or 5 GHz frequency spectrum is divided into evenly distributed chunks within the band as individual channels, each country having a regulatory domain that releases a certain amount of channels in each frequency spectrum.

2.2.2.6 Behaviour of radio waves

There are a few basic rules when it comes to radio waves. Longer waves, i.e. those with a lower frequency, can pass through obstacles and reach greater distances, but they have a more limited capacity for transmitting data, while the shorter the wavelength, the more data it transmits.

2.2.2.7 Absorption

The moment electromagnetic waves penetrate something they weaken or disappear, the level of power loss varies according to the frequency of the wave and the material it penetrates. In the case of microwaves used in wireless networks, the two main absorbent materials are metals and water, meaning that radio waves are unable to pass through them (FLICKENGER et al., 2007).

In the case of wood and trees, the level of absorption depends on the amount of water they contain, while plastics or similar are not usually absorbent. Human beings, because they have a large amount of water in their bodies, are highly absorbent, so wireless network design must take into account the number of people in a given environment (FLICKENGER et al., 2008).

2.2.2. 8Reflection

Like light, radio waves are reflected when they come into contact with suitable materials. The main sources of reflective material are metals and water surfaces. The angle at which the wave hits the material is the same as the angle at which it is reflected, as shown in Figure 3.

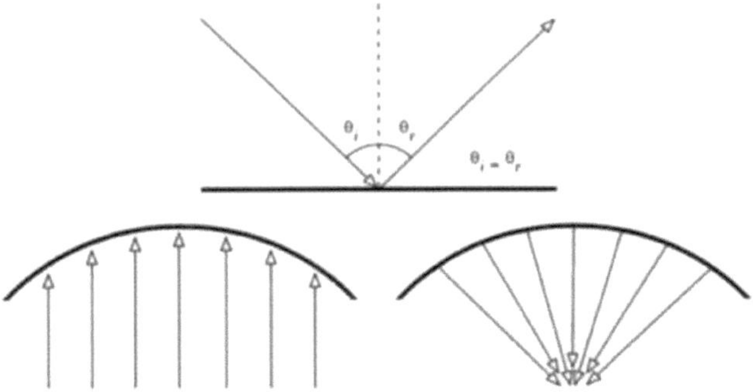

Figure 3 - Reflection of radio waves

Source: FLICKENGER et al. (2007, p. 18).

Offices, homes and even the outdoors are made up of countless metallic materials of different sizes and shapes, so it is extremely difficult to calculate where and with what intensity the electromagnetic waves will propagate. Despite the damage that reflection causes to wireless networks, it is used in the construction of some antennas, using parabolas behind the transmitter or receiver to concentrate the signal at an ideal point (FLICKENGER et al., 2007).

2.2.2.9 Interference

In wireless technology, interference is disturbance caused by other sources of radio frequencies, such as equipment working in the same spectrum or even other wireless networks with nearby channels. Interference

are the main sources of problems in wireless networks, especially in urban environments and indoor locations, where many networks can compete for the use of the same spectrum (FLICKENGER et al., 2007).

In wireless networks, interference can significantly impair transmission capacity, or even make it impossible to use Wi-Fi in a particular location.

2.2.2.10 Power

Electromagnetic waves carry energy, and the amount of energy received in a given amount of time is called power. Power is fundamental for wireless networks to work, a minimum amount of power is required for the receiver to recognise the signal (FLICKENGER et al., 2007).

2.2.3 Wireless network capacity

In wireless networks, and in this study in particular, some of the indicators that will be used to compare the efficiency of networks using different protocols are outlined below.

2.2.3.1 Signal level

Signal level is a measure in decibels (dB) that defines how much signal there is on a wireless link from an access point (transmitter) to one or more receivers. Each network has a minimum signal level to operate, but it must be in a specific signal range for its full capacity to be reached (FLICKENGER et al., 2007).

The signal level depends on numerous factors; what specification of transmitter and receiver is being used, what type of antenna the link has for both transmission and reception, how far away the devices are and what the level of interference is in the environment.

The signal originates in a transmitter and, until it reaches the receiver, is degraded by the loss of energy along the transmission path. It is necessary to take into account free space loss, attenuation and signal spreading. The greater the distance between the radios, the less signal is received due to free space loss (FLICKENGER et al., 2007).

The second contribution to signal degradation is loss through attenuation, which occurs because the signal power is absorbed when it passes through solid objects such as walls, windows and floors. Attenuation can vary greatly depending on the material in which the signal is absorbed, so it is very difficult to measure the amount of attenuation in a given environment (FLICKENGER et al., 2007).

Another factor that degrades the signal is scattering. As soon as the signal leaves the transmitter, part of it reaches the receiver's antenna directly, but another part hits other objects and is reflected, and part of this reflected energy also reaches the receiving antenna; this effect is called multipath, or signal dispersion. In some cases the reflected signals add up without causing problems, in other cases the signal can be cancelled out and impair the capacity of the link (FLICKENGER et al., 2007).

2.2.3.2 *Throughput*

Throughput measures the capacity of the wireless network, measured in *bits, in* a given time. In other words, the amount of data transmitted from one point to another in a given amount of time. Each *IEEE 802.11* protocol has its own maximum *throughput* specifications, but numerous factors influence *link* capacity (FLICKENGER et al., 2007).

The first factor that must be taken into account is the frequency used in the link. Higher frequencies have greater bandwidth transmission capacity than lower frequencies, but suffer more from signal attenuation in

indoor environments.

Another factor is the interference present in the radio frequency spectrum, since interference-laden environments can considerably reduce the network's capacity or even render it unusable.

The evolution of wireless network protocols has brought about a series of improvements in modulation, channel width and noise immunity, and bandwidth capacity *(throughput)* has grown exponentially with the emergence of new technologies and standards.

2.2.3.3 Latency

Data transmission is divided into packets and the time it takes for a packet to leave the transmitter and reach the receiver is latency, the lower it is, the better the Wi-Fi link, but it is not the only factor that defines network capacity (FLICKENGER et al., 2007).

A full-capacity wireless network must fulfil the specifications of; signal level within the recommended range, adequate *throughput* and consequently low latency.

CHAPTER 3

METHOD

This chapter presents the methodological procedures adopted to achieve the objectives set out in this work.

Barros and Lehfeld (2007) say that methodology is responsible for studying and analysing the different methods available, examining and evaluating research techniques. To this end, the methodological framework proposed for this study is presented in Chart 1, based on the specific literature of researchers Aaker, Kumar and Day (2011), Gil (2008;2012), Yin (2010), Barros and Lehfeld (2007), Beuren (2006), Malhotra (2001), Marconi and Lakatos (2010).

Table 1 - Methodological framework

Classification	Framework
Objectives	Descriptive/Exploratory
Nature	Applied
Scientific Method	Inductive
Approach	Qualitative/Quantitative
Technical procedures	Case studies

Source: prepared by the author.

1.1 Type of research

Research is defined by Marconi and Lakatos (2010, p. 139) as "a

a formal procedure, with a method of reflective thought, which requires **scientific treatment". The authors emphasise that research makes it possible to discover data** or facts, relationships or laws in any field of knowledge, and its realisation requires dedication, persistence, patience and continuous effort on the part of the researcher.

This research is classified as applied research. According to the authors Barros and Lehfeld (2007), applied research is motivated by the need to produce knowledge for the application of its results, aimed at the more or less immediate solution of a problem encountered in reality.

3.1.1 Defining the research in terms of its objectives

According to the objectives of this study, the research is **characterised as exploratory. According to Beuren (2006, p. 81)** "exploring a subject can mean gathering more knowledge, incorporating **unknown** characteristics, as **well as looking for new procedures".**

Aaker, Kumar and Day (2011, p. 94) state that: "Exploratory research is used when seeking an understanding of the general nature of a problem, the possible alternative hypotheses and the relevant variables that need to be **considered."**

The main objective of exploratory research, according to Malhotra (2001, p. **106), "is to explore a problem or situation in order to provide criteria and understanding". The author adds that exploratory research is characterised by** flexibility and versatility in terms of methods, which are responsible for providing the researcher with sufficient knowledge and understanding to proceed with the research project.

According to Marconi and Lakatos (2010), an exploratory study has three purposes: to develop hypotheses, to increase the researcher's familiarity with an environment, fact or phenomenon in order to carry out more precise future research, or to modify concepts. They conclude by saying that a variety of procedures can be used to collect data, such as interviews, observation and others, without using probabilistic sampling techniques.

The study in question is classified as exploratory, as it will be applied in order to deepen the researcher's knowledge of the subject and thus obtain better results for analysing and concluding the research.

3.1.2 Definition of the research in terms of the nature of the approach

This research can be considered qualitative. According to Malhotra (2011), qualitative research is used to define the research problem or to develop ways of approaching it, generating hypotheses and identifying variables. The author adds that this type of research aims to provide the researcher with a clearer view of the context in which the problem is inserted, since qualitative research is often used to explain the results obtained by quantitative research.

According to Beuren (2006), studies using a qualitative methodology can describe the complexity of a given problem, analyse certain variables and understand and classify dynamic processes.

3.1.3 Definition of the research in terms of technical procedures.

To carry out this study, we decided to use the following technical procedures:

a) Bibliographical research

Beuren (2006) defines bibliographical research as research that explains a particular problem using published theoretical references. As for Gil (2012), bibliographical research is carried out using material that has already been prepared, mainly in books and scientific articles. The material used in the research covers all the references already published in relation to the subject of study.

According to Marconi and Lakatos (2010), the main purpose of bibliographical research is to provide the researcher with direct contact with all the bibliography already published on the subject to be researched, offering the means to define and resolve the issues at stake.

proposed problems.

b) Experimental Research

Experimental research consists of determining an object of study, selecting some variables that could influence it and defining ways of controlling and observing the effects that the variable produces on the object (GIL, 2008).

According to Marconi and Lakatos (2010), the purpose of experimental research is to demonstrate the viability of a particular technique or programme as a potential and viable solution for certain practical programmes.

c) Case studies

According to Beuren (2006), the case study is mainly characterised by the study of a single case. This study is used by researchers who want to deepen their knowledge of a particular case. According to Gil (2012), it is characterised by the in-depth and exhaustive study of one or more objects, in order to allow broad and detailed knowledge.

Yin (2010) summarises the case study method as a wide-ranging research strategy that uses planning logic to incorporate specific approaches to data collection and data analysis.

3.2 Unit of analysis

According to Gil (2012), the first procedure consists of delimiting the unit that constitutes the case under study. This can be a person, a family, a community, a set of relationships or processes or even a culture.

3.3 Data collection plan

According to Marconi and Lakatos (2010), data collection corresponds to the stage of the research in which the application of the prepared instruments and selected techniques begins, with the aim of collecting the planned data. It requires patience, perseverance and personal effort on the part of the researcher, as well as care in recording the data and good prior preparation. The authors also point out that there are various techniques by which data can be collected, so it is important that the researcher has defined exactly which procedures they will use to avoid wasting time and facilitate their study.

Data collection, according to Barros and Lehfeld (2000, p. 89), "means the phase of the research in which questions are asked and data on reality is obtained through the application of **techniques". The authors also emphasise that: "The choice of research instrument,** however, will depend on the type of information you wish to obtain or the type of object of study" (BARROS; LEHFELD, 2000, p. 89).

The data will be collected through bench tests, using tools and techniques for analysing the quality of wireless networks, such as signal level, latency, interference level and network capacity *(throughput)*.

3.4 Data analysis plan

Aaker, Kumar and Day (2001) point out that data analysis can be considered as a set of techniques and methods to be used in order to obtain information and discoveries in relation to the data collected, helping to obtain significant knowledge about the proposed topic.

Malhotra (2001, p. 387) adds that the main aim of analysing the **data is "to provide information that** helps to approach the problem under **study".**

The data collected in the bench tests will be analysed and compared with current wireless network technologies.

3.5 Limitations of the method

The limitations of the method exist and are part of practically every research study. Every method has possibilities and limitations, so it is healthy for researchers to anticipate the criticisms that the reader may make of the work, explaining the limitations that the chosen method offers, but which still make it the most appropriate for the purposes of the investigation (VERGARA, 2007).

CHAPTER 4

CASE STUDY

This chapter describes how the case study was carried out. Sections 4.1, 4.2 and 4.3 describe respectively: the test environment, the transceivers used and the other equipment and tools that were required, section 4.4 defines the measurement and presentation of the data, while section 4.5 defines the test script used in each scenario.

4.1 The test environment

In order to provide maximum impartiality in the testing of each protocol, a single location was defined where all the scenarios were tested: an internal plan room of approximately 51 metres^2 made up of masonry walls, as shown in Figure 4.

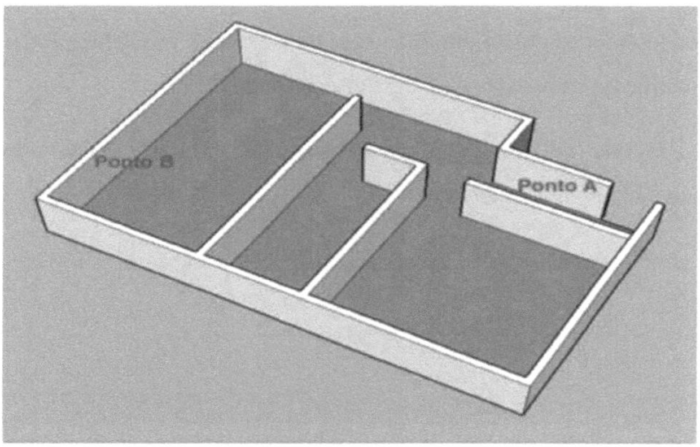

Figure 4 - Test environment layout
Source: prepared by the author.

The equipment used in the tests was installed at two points, A representing the Access Point and B the Receiver.

4.2Transceivers used

The transceivers were responsible for establishing the wireless network link between point A and B of the test environment, and it is in them that the protocol to be tested in each scenario is configured.

Once again, in order to obtain unbiased results, symmetrical transceivers from the same manufacturer were used in each test, but I didn't have access to a single transceiver model capable of operating in all wireless network protocols, so two models of equipment with similar technical characteristics were used in the tests.

These are radio frequency transceivers with integrated antennas, one of which operates and was therefore used to test 802.11b/g/n protocols at 2.4 GHz, the other was used to test 802.11a/n/ac protocols at 5.8 GHz. Below are the technical characteristics of each device:

Table 1 - Technical characteristics of the transceivers

Model	MikrotikSXT2	MikrotikSXT 5 AC
Supported protocols	802.11 b/g/n	802.11 a/n/ac
Operating frequency	2.4 GHz	5.8 GHz
Number of aerials	2	2
Antenna gain	10 Dbi	16 Dbi

Source: Prepared by the author.

The transceivers have two integrated antennas, one of which is vertically polarised and the other horizontally polarised. The protocols that use and benefit from two antennas to propagate the radio frequency are 802.11 n and ac, while the others only use one antenna for propagation.

It should be noted that the equipment operating on the 5.8 GHz frequency has antennas with a higher gain. This difference will be compensated for by adjusting the EIRP power in the transceiver used in each scenario. All the tests were carried out on the basis of ANATEL (National Telecommunications Agency) standards, so the channel and power adjustments strictly followed what the institution regulates as legal.

4.3 Equipment and analysis tools used

In addition to the transceivers, other equipment and tools were needed to measure the data in each scenario.

The tests were divided into two stages, one of which sought to extract technical results in terms of the performance of wireless network protocols, while the second has test results that are more applicable to corporate, academic or residential environments, so practical tests that are easy for ordinary users to understand.

In order to obtain the necessary technical performance information and then compare it, two pieces of equipment were used, one the Router 1 connected to the Access Point and the other the Router 2 connected to the Receiver, as shown in Figure 5.

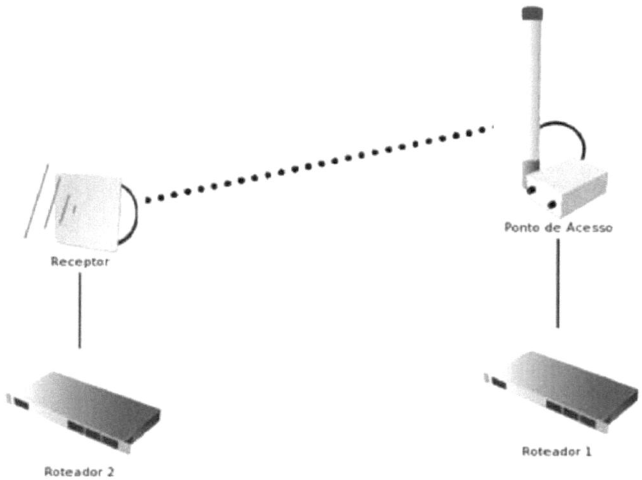

Figure 5 - Network 1 diagram

Source: prepared by the author.

These routers have tools that generate traffic for measuring link capacity, as well as analysing quality aspects such as latency and *throughput. The* tools used for these measurements were:

• *Mikrotik Badwith Test:* responsible for generating *UDP* packet traffic between Router 1 and Router 2.

• *Mikrotik Ping Tool:* responsible for analysing the latency of the *link* between Router 1 and Router 2, using a very common utility in computer networks, *ping* (Packet Internet Network Grouper).

Other technical information such as signal level and noise level will be extracted from the transceiver located at point A of the test environment.

For the second stage of more practical tests, an *FTP/Streaming* server connected to Router 1 and a computer connected to Router 2 were added to the network, which were responsible for the file *download* and *upload tests as* well as the video streaming test. For the last VOIP call test, two IP telephones capable of making direct IP calls were added to the network. The complete network diagram is shown in Figure 6.

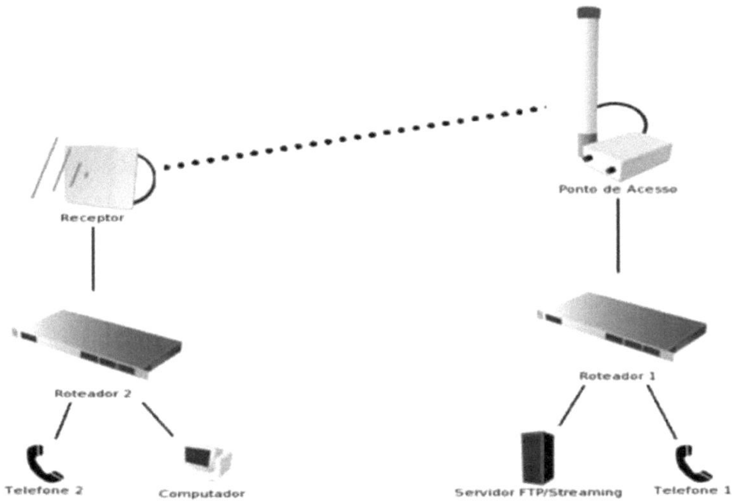

Figura 6 - Network diagram 2

Source: Prepared by the author.

4.4 Measuring and displaying data

In order to make it easier to understand how the data generated was captured and measured, each test carried out on the wireless network protocols is described below.

The first piece of information generated by the tests was extracted from the transceiver located at point A, the signal level of the link established in each scenario. This information does not directly represent a performance characteristic, it only serves to gauge the signal quality of the link, which in turn influences the performance capacity of each protocol.

For the first test of each protocol, the *throughput* analysis, the Mikrotik Badwith Test tool was used, which generated UDP packet traffic between Router 1 and Router 2 for 10 minutes. At the end of the test, the maximum *throughput and* average *throughput* data expressed in *Mbps (Megabits* per second) were collected. The most relevant information, and therefore the one that will be taken into account when analysing the results, is the average *throughput,* since it best represents the capacity of a *link* in a given time, the higher the *throughput the* better the protocol performance.

Along with the *throughput* test, the *Mikroitk Ping Tool* was used to measure the maximum and average latency values for each protocol in ms (milliseconds), as well as the percentage of packet loss. The most relevant information, and therefore the information used to analyse performance, was average latency and packet loss, where the lower the latency and packet loss, the better the protocol's performance.

For the file *download* test, a generic file of exactly 1 GB hosted on the *FTP/Streaming* server was used. The performance measurement took into account the time in minutes that each protocol needs to transmit the file from the server to the computer, which characterises a file *download,* where the shorter the time, the better the *link* capacity.

The *upload* test was carried out in a similar way to the previous one, but in the opposite direction, measuring the time in minutes required for each protocol to transmit a file of exactly 1 GB from the computer to the *FTP/Streaming* server, characterising file *uploads.*

The purpose of the video *streaming* test was to analyse the ability of each wireless network protocol tested to transmit 31-minute videos in *SD,* another in *FullHD* and another in *4K*, from the *FTP/Streaming* server to the computer. The performance measurement was visual and was based on the ability to transmit the videos without cuts or delays in the image or sound, so each protocol received a score from 1 to 5 for each type of video transmitted, where 1 is the total inability to transmit and 5 is the ability to transmit the video smoothly. Alongside the transmission of the videos in each scenario, a latency test was carried out to measure packet loss during transmission.

For the VOIP call test, two telephones with direct IP call technology were used. During a 10-minute call on each protocol, the audio transmission capacity was analysed without cuts, delays or echoes.To evaluate the protocols in terms of video streaming and VOIP calls, the parameterisation suggested by Siluk (2007, p. 101) was used as a basis, as shown in Table 2.

Table 2 - Evaluation criteria (Adaptation of the signalling metaphor)

Totally dissatisfied	Stop such a dissatisfied mind	Satisfied	Partially satisfied	Fully satisfied
	2	3	4	5
Low level of fulfilment of the item or factor	Insufficient fulfilment of the item or factor	Moderate fulfilment of the item or factor	Sufficient fulfilment of the item or factor	High level of fulfilment of the item or factor
Does not fulfil the requirement	It's unacceptable, but it fulfils part of the requirement	Acceptable with reservations	Moderately meets the requirement	Fully meets the requirement
Not very important	Insignificant degree of importance	Moderate degree of importance	Important	Very important
Oa 20%	21 a 40%	41 a 60%	61 a 80%	SI to 100

Source: Adapted by the author from Siluk (2007).

To meet the needs of the tests, the evaluation options were parameterised, as shown in Table 3.

Table 3 - Options for evaluating criteria

Value	Transmission option
5	Total capacity (excellent)
4	Good capacity
3	Average capacity
2	Low capacity
1	Total disability (Bad)

Source: Adapted by the author from Funke (2015).

4.5 Test script

Based on the information on transceivers, equipment, tools and data measurement, it was possible to create a test script to ensure the integrity and impartiality of the data generated by the scenarios, the script was applied to each protocol tested, the procedures follow in order:

- Installation of the transceivers at point A and B of the test environment;
- Configuration of the transceivers in the protocol to be tested;
- Spectrum analysis to obtain the channel with the lowest noise level within the environment;
- Check the signal level obtained on the link;
- Connect Router 1 to the Access Point and Router 2 to the Receiver;
- Perform the *throughput* test between Router 1 and Router 2;
- Perform a latency test between Router 1 and Router 2;
- Connect the *FTP/Streaming* server to the Router 1;
- Connect the computer to the router 2;
- Start the test of downloading files from the server to the computer;
- Start the test of *uploading* files from the computer to the server;
- Start the SD quality video *streaming* test between the server and the computer;
- Start the test by *streaming* video in *FullHD* quality between the server and the computer;
- Start the 4K video *streaming* test between the server and the computer;
- Connect the *VOIP* phones to routers 1 and 2;
- Start the *VOIP* call test between the phones;

In order to demonstrate the integrity and topology of the network used in each scenario, external access to the controlled network was necessary to validate the operation of the equipment used in the tests. To do this, a ping test was carried out to a server hosted on the Internet before initialising the internal tests on each protocol.

CHAPTER 5

ANALYSING THE DATA

The aim of this chapter is to analyse and compare the data obtained from the test scenarios in order to reach conclusions that are relevant to the research objective.

5.1 Scenario 1 - 802.11b protocol

The first scenario aimed to test the performance of the 802.11b protocol. The transceivers used for the tests were Mikrotik SXT 2s, whose technical characteristics are shown in Table 2.

According to the test script, the first step was to install the symmetrical transceivers at points A and B as shown in Figure 4, which were configured to operate only on the 802.11b protocol. Although the environment had no other equipment operating on the 2.4 GHz frequencies, the Mikrotik Frequency Usage tool was used to analyse the radio frequency spectrum in search of a particular frequency with the lowest noise level; after analysis, the frequency chosen was 2447 Mhz in 20 Mhz of bandwidth.

With the link established, the signal level extracted from the transceiver at point A was -61 dB. Once the scenario was set up, the other equipment was added as necessary and the tests began according to the test script, the results of which are shown below.The first *throughput and* latency tests went without a hitch and obtained the results shown in Table 4.

Table 4 - Tests on the Mikrotik SXT 2 device (802.11b - 2.4 GHz)

Variable	Value
Average throughput	6.5 Mbps
Maximum throughput	6.8 Mbps
Average latency	431 ms
Maximum latency	492 ms
Minimum latency	415 ms
Packet loss	0%

Source: prepared by the author.

We can see that after 10 minutes of testing, the average *throughput* was 6.5 Mbps, the average latency was 431 ms and packet loss was 0%.

The file download test took 24:37 minutes to complete, while the upload test was completed in 26:21 minutes.

Table 5 shows the results of the video streaming tests.

Table 5 - Video evaluation - Mikrotik SXT 2 (802.11b - 2.4 GHz)

Video quality	SD	FULLHD	4K
Note	5	2	1
Packet loss	0%	65%	88%

Source: prepared by the author.

The 802.11b protocol received top marks when transmitting *SD* videos, with no problems during transmission. However, it was unable to transmit *FullHD* video smoothly, with several image and sound cuts during the 31 minutes of transmission, which earned it a score of 2. The inability to start transmission of a *4K* video resulted in a minimum score in this area.

The test, which aimed to analyse the quality of a *VOIP* call between two phones, went smoothly for 10 minutes, so in this test the 802.11b protocol received a score of 5.

5.2 Scenario 2 - 802.11a protocol

For the second scenario, the Mikrotik SXT 5 AC transceiver was used, which will also be used for testing the 802.11n protocols at 5.8 GHz and 802.11ac. Its technical characteristics are shown in Table 1. Based on the test script, the first step was to install the transceivers at points A and B in the test environment and configure them to operate only on the 802.11a protocol. According to the Frequency Usage tool, the frequency with the lowest noise in the environment was 5870 MHz, which is therefore the frequency used in the test. With the link established, the signal extracted from the transceiver at point A was -57 dB.

As necessary, the other equipment was added to the scenario and the tests started according to the pre-established script, the results of which are shown below.

The first *throughput and* latency tests went without a hitch during the 10 minutes, and the results are shown in Table 6.

Chart 6 - Tests on the Mikrotik SXT 5 AC device (802.11a - 5.8 GHz)

Variable	Value
Average throughput	28.3 Mbps
Maximum throughput	29.0 Mbps
Average latency	83 ms
Maximum latency	89 ms
Minimum latency	81 ms
Packet loss	0,00%

Source: prepared by the author.

The table shows that the average *throughput* was 28.3 Mbps, the average latency was 83 ms and packet loss was 0 per cent.

It took 05:47 minutes to download the 1 GB file and 05:59 minutes to upload it.

Table 7 shows the scores during the video streaming tests.

Table 7 - Video evaluation - Mikrotik SXT 5 AC (802.11a - 5.8Ghz)

Video quality	SD	FULLHD	4K
Note	5	5	2
Packet loss	0%	0%	61%

Source: prepared by the author.

The 802.11a protocol provided the necessary capacity to perfectly execute the SD video, so it got a score of 5. The same occurred with the FullHD video, but in the 4K streaming test, the protocol was unable to maintain the transmission that started and in a few seconds stopped and could no longer be resumed, which earned it a score of 2.

The VOIP call test went without any delays, cuts or echoes, so a score of 5.

5.3Scenario 3 - 802.11g protocol

The third scenario aimed to test the 802.11g protocol, so Mikrotik SXT 2 transceivers were used.

With the equipment installed at points A and B in the test environment, they were configured to operate only on the 802.11g protocol, and the spectrum analysis again revealed the 2447 MHz frequency, with 20 MHz of bandwidth, with the lowest noise level, and therefore the one used in the tests.

The link established revealed a signal level of -62 dB from transceiver A. The other equipment was then added as necessary to start the tests according to the script, and the results are shown below.

The 10-minute *throughput and* latency tests went without a hitch and the results are shown in Table 8.

Table 8 - Tests on the Mikrotik SXT 2 device (802.11 g - 2.4 GHz)

Variable	Value
Average throughput	26.6 Mbps
Maximum throughput	28.5 Mbps
Average latency	103 ms
Maximum latency	126 ms
Minimum latency	97 ms
Packet loss	0%

Source: prepared by the author.

After 10 minutes of testing, the average *throughput* was 26.6 Mbps, the average latency was 103 ms and packet loss was 0 per cent.

Following the script, the file download test was completed in 05:57 minutes, while the upload test took 06:12 minutes to complete.

Table 9 shows the results of the visual test of streaming videos in different image qualities.

Table 9 - Video evaluation - Mikrotik SXT 2 (802.11g - 2.4 GHz)

Video quality	SD	FULLHD	4K
Note	5	4	2
Packet loss	0%	8%	64%

Source: prepared by the author.

Visual analysis during video *streaming* revealed that the 802.11g protocol is capable of transmitting videos in *SD* quality without any problems, so it received a score of 5. During the *FullHD video* test, there was only one video crash which was re-established shortly afterwards, so it received a score of *4. The* protocol did not do well during *4K video transmission*, seconds after the start of transmission, the video was interrupted and the protocol was no longer able to provide the necessary capacity to resume transmission.

As in the previous scenarios, the 802.11g protocol had no problems providing an IP voice call between the two phones, so it scored a 5 in this test.

5.4 Scenario 4 - 802.11 n protocol at 2.4 Ghz

One of the characteristics of the 802.11n protocol is the ability to operate at 2.4 GHz or 5.8 GHz, so we will have two test scenarios for this protocol. In the first of these, the Mikroitk SXT 2 transceiver was used, the same one used in the previous scenario, but this time configured to operate only on the 802.11n protocol at 2.4 GHz with 40 MHz of bandwidth. Spectrum analysis with the Frequency Usage tool revealed the 2447 MHz frequency with the lowest noise level in the environment, which is why it was used in the tests. The signal level obtained on the link was -62 dB.

Once the transceivers were installed, the other equipment was added to the scenario as needed to carry out the tests according to the script, and the results are shown below.

The first *throughput and* latency tests went without a hitch and revealed the data in Table 10.

Table 10 - Tests on the Mikrotik SXT 2 device (802.11 n - 2.4 GHz)

Variable	Value
Average throughput	161.9 Mbps
Maximum throughput	199.7 Mbps
Average latency	15 ms
Maximum latency	60 ms
Minimum latency	5 ms
Packet loss	0%

Source: prepared by the author.

The average *throughput of* the 802.11n protocol at 2.4 GHz was

161.9 Mbps, the average latency during the test was 15 ms, there were no packet losses.

The time taken to download the 1 GB file was 02:35 minutes, and the time taken to upload the same file was 02:17 minutes.

Table 11 shows the results of the video streaming tests.

Table 11 - Video evaluation - Mikrotik SXT 2 (802.11n - 2.4 GHz)

Video quality	SD	FULLHD	4K
Note	5	5	5
Packet loss	0%	0%	0%

Source: prepared by the author.

The 802.11n protocol at 2.4 GHz was able to provide enough capacity for SD, FullHD and 4K videos to run smoothly, so it scored 5 in all the streaming tests.

The VOIP call test was also carried out without any problems and once again the protocol scored 5.

5.5 Scenario 5 - 802.11 n protocol at 5.8 Ghz

After testing the 802.11n protocol at 2.4 GHz, the scenario for testing the same protocol was run, but at a frequency of 5.8 GHz, so the transceivers used in this test were Mikrotik SXT 5 AC, installed at points A and B in the test environment, revealing a signal level of -58 dB using the 5870 MHz frequency at 40 MHz of bandwidth, since the Frequency Usage tool revealed it to have the lowest noise level in the environment.

With the transceivers installed and configured, the other equipment was added as required according to the test script, the results of which are shown below.

The first *throughput* and latency tests went smoothly and revealed the results in Table 12.

Chart 12 - Tests on the Mikrotik SXT 5 AC device (802.11n - 5.8 GHz)

Variable	Value
Average throughput	204.6 Mbps
Maximum throughput	235.8 Mbps
Average latency	15 ms
Maximum latency	27 ms
Minimum latency	1 ms
Packet loss	0%

Source: prepared by the author.

Average *throughput* was 204.6 Mbps, average latency was 15 ms and there were no packet losses.

The time taken to download the 1 GB file was 00:56 seconds, the upload was completed in

01:10 minutes.

Table 13 shows the results for the video streaming tests.

Table 13 - Video evaluation - Mikrotik SXT 5 (802.11n - 5.8 GHz)

Video quality	SD	FULLHD	4K
Note	5	5	5
Packet loss	0%	0%	0%

Source: prepared by the author.

The 802.11n protocol at 5.8 GHz, as well as at 2.4 GHz, did not present any problems during the execution of videos in SD, FullHD and 4K, obtaining maximum marks in all the streaming tests.The VOIP call test also went without any problems and therefore scored 5.

5.6 Scenario 6 - 802.11AC protocol

The sixth and final scenario aimed to test the 802.11ac protocol, based on the test script, the first step was to install the transceivers at points A and B of the test environment, after which they were configured to operate only in the 802.11ac protocol, once again the transceiver used was the Mikrotik SXT 5 AC, the frequency chosen, based on the Frequency Usage tool was 5870 MHz in 80 MHz of bandwidth.

The signal level obtained on the link was -59 dB, to the extent necessary, the other equipment was installed and the tests started according to the script, the results are shown below.

The *throughput and* latency tests went without a hitch and the results are shown in Table 14.

Chart 14 - Tests on the Mikrotik SXT 5 AC (802.11 ac - 5.8 GHz) device

Variable	Value
Average throughput	298.8 Mbps
Maximum throughput	363.6 Mbps
Average latency	10 ms
Maximum latency	19 ms
Minimum latency	1 ms
Packet loss	0%

Source: prepared by the author.

According to the table above, the average *throughput* was 298.8 Mbps, the average latency was 10 ms and there were no packet losses.

During the download test, the protocol needed 00:41 seconds to complete the transfer of the 1 GB file, while the upload time for the same file was 00:47 seconds.

Table 15 shows the protocol scores for the streaming test.

Table 15 - Video evaluation - Mikrotik SXT 5 AC (802.11ac - 5.8 GHz)

Video quality	SD	FULLHD	4K
Note	5	5	5
Packet loss	0%	0%	0%

Source: prepared by the author.

The 802.11ac protocol had no problems transmitting videos in SD, FullHD or 4K, so it scored top marks in all the streaming tests.

As in the previous test, the protocol provided a VOIP call without any delay, cuts or echoes in the audio, so it scored a 5.

5.7Analysing results

The following analyses the results obtained in the tests for each scenario, using graphs to help understand and compare the data generated.

The first test for each protocol, the *throughput* test, generated the following graph.

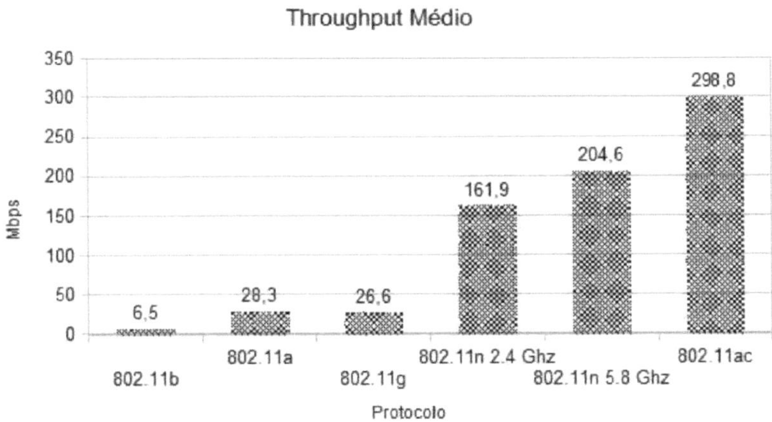

Graph 1 - Average Throughput

Source: prepared by the author.

The gain in *throughput* performance in wireless networks over time is evident; tests have revealed that the current 802.11ac protocol has 46 times more *throughput* capacity than the first protocol launched in mid-1999,

it can also be seen that there has been a significant gain in *throughput* capacity with the emergence of the 802.11n protocol compared to the protocols that preceded it.

Another important analysis is the superior *throughput of* protocols working at 5.8 GHz frequencies

The latency test, which was carried out alongside the *throughput* test for each protocol, generated the data shown in the graph below.

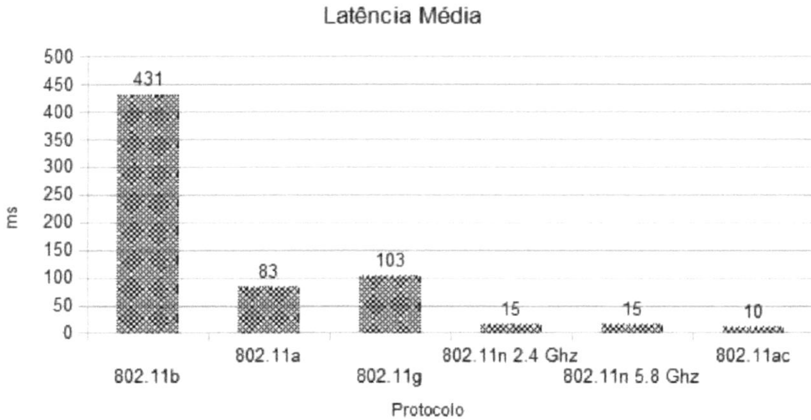

Graph 2 - Average Latency

Source: prepared by the author.

Although this information is not very relevant to the protocol's performance, it is clear from the graph that the quality of the protocols' latency has improved over time. The test of downloading a generic file of 1 GB in size showed the results expressed in minutes in the following graph.

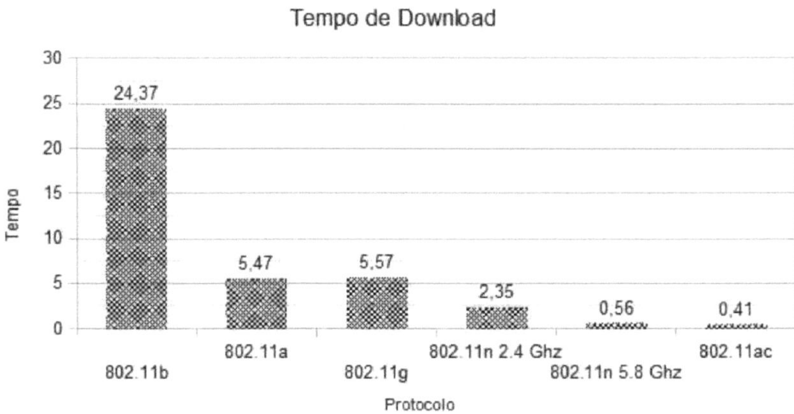

Graph 3 - Download time
Source: prepared by the author.

While the 802.11b protocol takes 24 minutes and 37 seconds to download a 1 GB file, the 802.11ac protocol only needed 41 seconds to download the same file, a 59-fold gain in download performance between the first and last protocols tested. Once again, protocols operating in 5.8 GHz frequency bands performed better than protocols operating in 2.4 GHz frequencies.

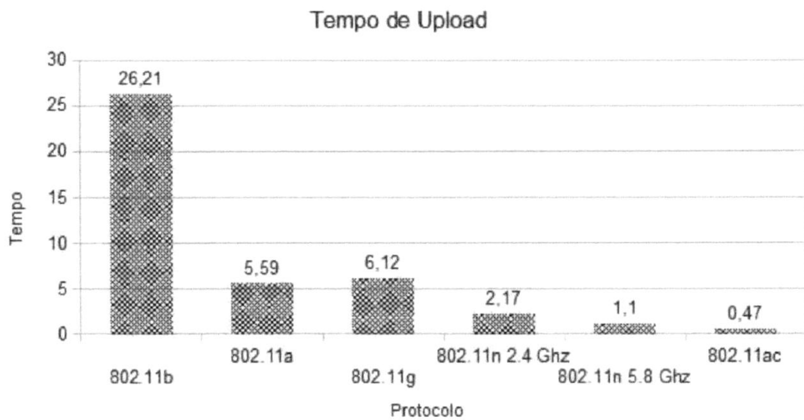

Graph 4 - Upload time
Source: prepared by the author.

Similar results to the download tests were obtained in the upload tests for the 1 GB file. Once again, the performance gains of the wireless network protocols over time were evident. The graphs below show the results of the video streaming tests for each protocol.

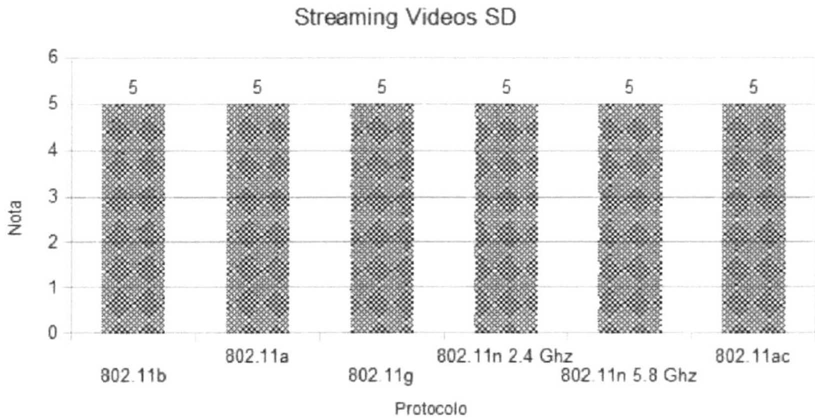

Graph 5 - Streaming SD videos

Source: prepared by the author.

All the protocols performed satisfactorily when transmitting videos in SD quality, which shows that any wireless network protocol tested in this study is capable of transmitting videos in reduced quality smoothly.

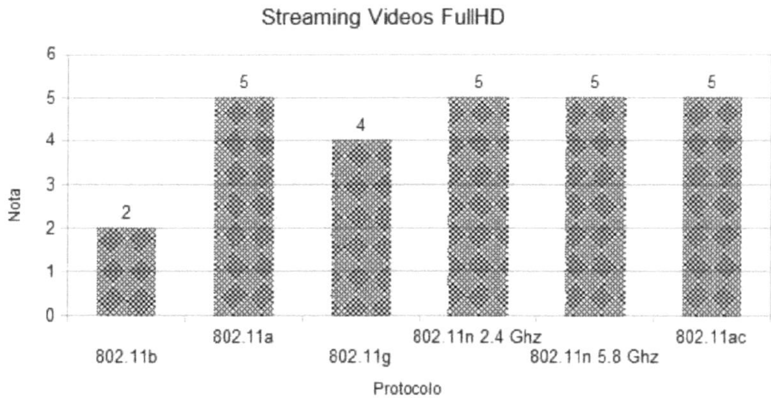

Graph 6 - Streaming FullHD videos

Source: prepared by the author.

During the FullHD video streaming test, the 802.11b protocol had performed poorly, followed by the 802.11g protocol which, due to a detail, did not get top marks, while the other protocols performed their function without problems, getting top marks.

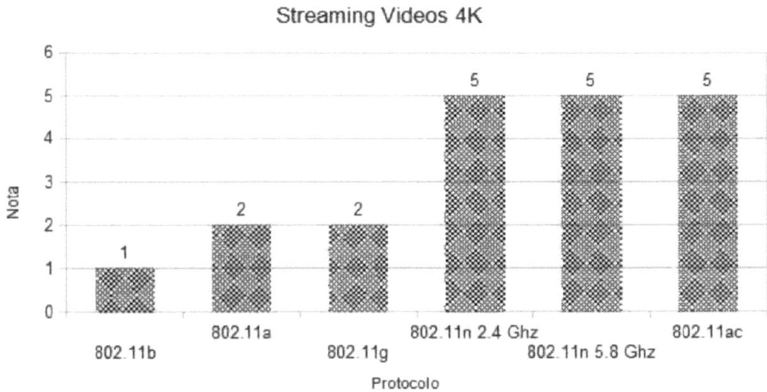

Graph 7 - Streaming 4K videos

Source: prepared by the author.

During the 4K video streaming tests, the only protocols that obtained satisfactory results were the 802.11n protocols at 2.4 or 5.8 GHz and the 802.11ac protocol, the others are not recommended for this type of application.The last test for each protocol, the VOIP call test, revealed the data in the table below.

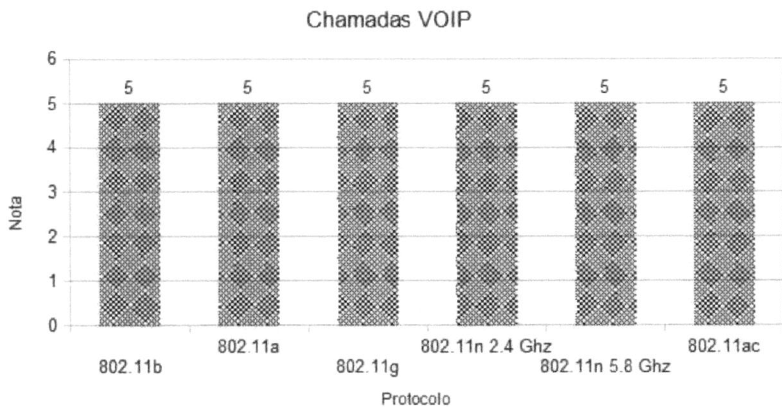

Graph 8 - VOIP calls

Source: prepared by the author.

For the VOIP call tests, all the protocols obtained satisfactory results; if the aim of the wireless network is to provide VOIP calls or similar applications, any protocol is capable of performing this task without problems.

Two appendices located at the end of the paper show the test results for each scenario in table format. Appendix A - Results Analysis, shows the data for the *throughput,* latency, *download* and *upload tests,* while Appendix B - Video Test Analysis, shows the results for the video tests for each protocol.

CHAPTER 6

CONCLUSION

The ever-increasing number of devices and applications that use the Internet demands ever greater capacity from wireless networks. This study set out to analyse the performance of each wireless network protocol whose equipment is commercially available on the market, and the tests revealed that the evolution of this technology over the years is evident.

The first specific objective of the study, to analyse the performance of each wireless network protocol, was successfully achieved, providing parameters for comparison and analysis between them.

For the second and third specific objective of the study, the comparison of the results of each protocol, it was found that for certain applications, the protocols with the lowest capacity are sufficient to provide the necessary fluidity, while when the applications demand more capacity, as in the case of streaming FullHD or 4K videos, more advanced wireless network protocols should be chosen that can provide more capacity.

It's important to emphasise that in order to have the full capacity of a given protocol, both pieces of equipment used in a wireless network must be compatible with it. There's no point in replacing a router, for example, if the notebook, smartphone or any other device isn't compatible with the protocol in which the router operates.

This study should help home users or wireless network managers decide whether to buy wireless equipment compatible with a particular protocol or another, depending on the level of performance that each network needs to provide in the environment.

For future work, we suggest analysing the performance of the protocols on point-to-multipoint links, as well as using equipment from different manufacturers, which would further enrich the comparison study between wireless network protocols.

REFERENCES

AAKER, D. A.; KUMAR, V.; DAY, G. S. **Marketing research.** São Paulo: Atlas, 2011.

BARROS, Aidil J. da Silveira; LEHFELD, Neide A. de Souza. **Fundamentals of scientific methodology**: a guide to scientific initiation. São Paulo: Makron Books, 2000.

BEUREN, Ilse Maria. **How to Write Accounting Monographs:** Theory and Practice. 3. ed., São Paulo, 2006.

CHEMIN, Beatris Francisca. **Univates manual for academic work**: planning, preparation and presentation. 3. ed. Lajeado: ed. Univates, 2015.

FLICKENGER, Rob et al. **Wireless networks in the developing world**. 2. ed. Hacker Friendly, 2007.

FOROUZAN, Behrouz A. **Data communications and computer networks.** 4- ed. São Paulo: Mc Graw Hil, 2008.

FUNKE, E. **Modelling performance measurement based on customer satisfaction at BRASILATA S/A**. Master's dissertation (Postgraduate Programme in Production Engineering). Federal University of Santa Maria, Santa Maria, 2015.

GIL, Antonio C. **Métodos e técnicas de pesquisa social**. 6. ed. São Paulo: Atlas, 2012.

MARCONI, Marina de A.; LAKATOS, Eva M. **Fundamentos de metodologia científica**. 7. ed. São Paulo: Atlas, 2010.

MALHOTRA, Naresh K. **Marketing research**: focus on the decision. 3. ed. São Paulo: Pearson, 2011.

MORAES, Alexandre Fernades de. **Wireless networks:** Installation, configuration and security. 1. ed. São Paulo: Erica, 2010.

PLAZA, William R. **Understanding Wi-Fi 802.11ac.** Available at: <http://www.hardware.com.br/artigos/entendendo-Wi-Fi-802.11-ac/>. Accessed on: 11 October 2015.

SILUK, J. M. **Organisational management model based on a performance evaluation system**. 2007. 176f. PhD Thesis (Postgraduate Programme in Production Engineering). Federal University of Santa Catarina, Florianópolis, 2007.

TANENBAUM, Andrew S.,WETHERALL, David. **Computer networks.** 5th edition. São Paulo: Pearson, 2011.

VERGARA, Sylvia C. **Research projects and reports in administration**. 9. ed. São Paulo: Atlas, 2007.

YIN, Robert K. **Case Study**: Planning and Methods. 4. ed. Porto Alegre: Bookman, 2010.

APPENDICES

APPENDIX A - Analysis of results

Scenarios	1	2	3	4	5	6
Equipment	Mikrotik SXT 2	Mikrotik SXT 5 AC	Mikrotik SXT 2	Mikrotik SXT 2	Mikrotik SXT 5 AC	Mikrotik SXT 5 AC
Protocol	802.11b	802.11a	802.11g	802.11n	802.11n	802.11AC
Frequency	2.4Ghz	5.8Ghz	2.4Ghz	2.4 Ghz	5.8Ghz	5.8Ghz
Variable	Values					
Average throughput	6.5 Mbps	28.3 Mbps	26.6 Mbps	161.9 Mbps	204.6 Mbps	298.8 Mbps
Maximum throughput	6.8 Mbps	29.0 Mbps	28.5 Mbps	199.7 Mbps	235.8 Mbps	363.6 Mbps
Average latency	431 ms	83 ms	103 ms	15 ms	15 ms	10 ms
Maximum latency	492 ms	89 ms	126 ms	60 ms	27 ms	19 ms
Minimum latency	415 ms	81 ms	97 ms	5 ms	1 ms	1 ms

Packet loss	0%	0%	0%	0%	0%	0%
Download 1 Gb	24:37	5:47	5:57	2:35	0:56	0:41
Upload 1 Gb	26:21	5:59	6:12	2:17	1:10	0:47

APPENDIX B - Analysing the Video Test

Scenarios	**1**	**2**	**3**	**4**	**5**	**6**
Equipment	Mikrotik SXT 2	Mikrotik SXT 5 AC	Mikrotik SXT 2	Mikrotik SXT 2	Mikrotik SXT 5 AC	Mikrotik SXT 5 AC
Protocol	802.11b	802.11a	802.11g	802.11n	802.11n	802.11AC
Frequency	2.4 Ghz	5.8 Ghz	2.4 Ghz	2.4 Ghz	5.8 Ghz	5.8 Ghz
Video format	**Notes on Video Quality**					
SD	5	5	5	5	5	5
FULLHD	2	5	4	5	5	5
4K	1	2	2	5	5	5
	Results					
	8	12	11	15	15	15

MIX
Papier aus verantwortungsvollen Quellen
Paper from responsible sources
FSC® C105338

Printed by Books on Demand GmbH, Norderstedt / Germany